ELENA CARINA MENDOZA

Journey Through Nicaragua

Your Essential Guide to Top Attractions, Local Customs, and Must-See Activities for the Trip of a Lifetime

Copyright © 2023 by Elena Carina Mendoza

All rights reserved. No part of this publication may be reproduced, stored or transmitted in any form or by any means, electronic, mechanical, photocopying, recording, scanning, or otherwise without written permission from the publisher. It is illegal to copy this book, post it to a website, or distribute it by any other means without permission.

Elena Carina Mendoza asserts the moral right to be identified as the author of this work.

Elena Carina Mendoza has no responsibility for the persistence or accuracy of URLs for external or third-party Internet Websites referred to in this publication and does not guarantee that any content on such Websites is, or will remain, accurate or appropriate.

Designations used by companies to distinguish their products are often claimed as trademarks. All brand names and product names used in this book and on its cover are trade names, service marks, trademarks and registered trademarks of their respective owners. The publishers and the book are not associated with any product or vendor mentioned in this book. None of the companies referenced within the book have endorsed the book.

First edition

This book was professionally typeset on Reedsy.
Find out more at reedsy.com

"Nicaragua is becoming the least expensive Caribbean destination."

— Arthur Frommer

Contents

1	Introduction	1
2	Pre-Trip Planning and What To Expect	5
3	Getting Settled Once You Arrive	19
4	The Foods of Nicaragua	29
5	Best Hikes	40
6	Best Beaches	55
7	Day Trips	68
8	Best Family Activities	77
9	Best Surf Spots	82
10	Conclusion	87
11	Resources	91
	About the Author	93

1

Introduction

Welcome to your essential guide for exploring Nicaragua. This book is designed as a practical tool to help you navigate through the unique experiences Nicaragua offers, combining adventure with cultural immersion. My role is to be your practical guide, sharing insights from my extensive travels in Nicaragua to enhance your journey.

Nicaragua is an emerging destination, offering a blend of natural beauty, rich history, and an authentic experience that is becoming increasingly rare in more tourist-heavy locales. It's a choice for the discerning

INTRODUCTION

traveler who values rich experiences over mere sightseeing.

This guide is tailored for those who want an enriching vacation without breaking the bank. Nicaragua stands out for its affordability, offering a wealth of experiences that are both accessible and memorable. Whether you're traveling solo, with a partner, or with your family, this guide will serve as your compass.

In Chapter 2, "Pre-Trip Planning and What To Expect," I'll provide you with essential information to prepare you for your trip. This includes understanding the best times to visit, cultural norms, and practical tips on currency, communication, and safety.

Chapter 3, "Getting Settled Once You Arrive," offers advice on how to navigate from the airport, find reliable transportation, and settle into your first day in Nicaragua with ease and confidence.

For food enthusiasts, Chapter 4, "The Foods of Nicaragua," is a concise guide to the must-try dishes and dining experiences, along with recommendations for the best local eateries and street food spots.

Chapters 5 and 6 are your guides to the outdoors. In "Best Hikes," I detail the top hiking trails for various skill levels, and in "Best Beaches," I highlight the most pristine and tranquil beaches for relaxation or adventure.

If you're looking to explore beyond the usual, Chapter 7, "Day Trips," provides a list of must-visit locations and activities that are perfect for a short excursion, offering a taste of Nicaragua's diversity.

Chapter 8, "Best Family Activities," focuses on ensuring that travelers of all ages have a memorable and engaging experience, highlighting activities that are both fun and family-friendly.

For surfers, Chapter 9, "Best Surf Spots," is a straightforward guide to the top surfing locations, suitable for beginners and experienced surfers alike, ensuring you catch the best waves Nicaragua has to offer.

Finally, the Conclusion will offer some final tips and advice to ensure your trip is not just enjoyable, but truly remarkable.

This book is your tool to navigate Nicaragua's hidden treasures. It's time to start your journey.

2

Pre-Trip Planning and What To Expect

E mbarking on a journey to Nicaragua requires thoughtful preparation to ensure your trip is as smooth and enjoyable as possible. This chapter is your practical roadmap for all the essentials you need to address before you set foot in this vibrant country. From booking flights to deciding the length of your stay, each subsection here is designed to provide you with concise, actionable advice.

Booking Your Flights

Booking your flight is the first step in your journey to Nicaragua, and getting the best deal requires a blend of strategy and timing. Start by comparing flight prices across various travel websites and airlines. Tools like Skyscanner or Google Flights are invaluable for this, offering a comprehensive view of available options. Generally, booking your flight several months in advance is a good rule of thumb for catching lower rates. However, don't overlook the potential for last-minute deals, as airlines sometimes drop prices to fill seats close to departure dates.

Most international travelers will find themselves landing at Augusto C. Sandino International Airport in Managua, Nicaragua's bustling capital. Major airlines such as American Airlines, United, and Avianca offer direct or connecting flights to Managua from various international cities. For those looking to minimize travel time and potential layover hassles, it's worth exploring routes with fewer stops. Also, consider regional carriers like Copa Airlines or local airlines like La Costeña for potentially more economical options, especially for regional travel within Central America.

A few lesser-known tips can also make a significant difference. Flying on weekdays can often result in cheaper fares compared to weekend travel. Regularly clearing your browser cookies or using an incognito mode might reveal lower flight prices due to the way airline pricing algorithms work. Additionally, subscribing to airline newsletters can alert you to special offers or limited-time sales, which can be a boon for budget-conscious travelers.

Finally, consider your arrival time in Nicaragua. Flights landing in the morning or early afternoon are ideal if you prefer to get settled or travel onwards from Managua before nightfall. A well-timed arrival can set a relaxed and comfortable tone for the start of your adventure in this beautiful country.

Arriving From Outside of Nicaragua

When you arrive in Nicaragua from an international destination, understanding the customs, immigration processes, and currency considerations is crucial for a seamless entry. As you disembark, typically at Augusto C. Sandino International Airport in Managua, your first encounter will be with immigration. The wait here can vary, but it's common to spend anywhere from a few minutes to about an hour in line, particularly during peak travel times. Ensure your passport is handy, and if you're from a country that necessitates a visa or a tourist card (not required for many nationalities for up to 90 days), be prepared to handle this upon arrival. Typically, a fee of around $10 USD is charged for visas or tourist cards, and it's important to carry this amount in cash, as credit card facilities might not be available at immigration counters.

Currency is an important consideration upon arrival. The Nicaraguan Córdoba (NIO) is the local currency, and while US dollars are accepted in many tourist areas, having local currency is advisable for smaller purchases, especially outside the main tourist spots. Exchange services are available at the airport, but you might find better rates at banks or authorized bureaus in the city.

After clearing immigration, you'll proceed to the baggage claim area, which is relatively easy to navigate due to the airport's modest size. While trolleys and porter services are available, keeping a close eye on your belongings is recommended. Following baggage collection, you'll undergo a final customs check, typically a swift process involving a scan of your bags.

PRE-TRIP PLANNING AND WHAT TO EXPECT

As you step into the main hall of the airport, you'll be greeted by a bustling atmosphere, with representatives from various hotels, tour companies, and taxi services. To avoid the initial rush, consider pre-arranging your transportation to your accommodation. Lastly, be prepared for Nicaragua's tropical climate; it's generally warm, with varying humidity levels across different regions. Light, breathable clothing is advisable, along with staying hydrated, especially after your flight.

This guide will help ensure your arrival in Nicaragua is as smooth and stress-free as possible, setting the tone for an enjoyable and memorable visit.

Budgeting for Your Trip

Budgeting for your Nicaraguan adventure requires a thoughtful approach to ensure your trip is both enjoyable and financially manageable. Nicaragua is known for its affordability, but like any destination, expenses can vary greatly depending on your travel preferences and lifestyle. Let's break down the key cost components: accommodation, food, transportation, and activities, to help you craft a budget that aligns with your travel goals.

- **Accommodation**: Your choice of accommodation in Nicaragua can significantly impact your budget. For budget travelers, hostels and guesthouses are plentiful, with prices ranging from $10 to $20 USD per night for a dorm bed or a basic private room. Mid-range options, including small hotels and B&Bs, typically cost between $30 and $60 USD per night and offer a balance of comfort and local charm. For those seeking luxury, upscale resorts or boutique

hotels can cost anywhere from $300 to over $400 USD per night, offering premium amenities and locations. When budgeting for accommodation, consider factors like location, included amenities (like breakfast or WiFi), and the type of experience you want.
- **Food**: Dining in Nicaragua is a diverse and affordable experience. Street food and local markets offer a chance to taste authentic Nicaraguan cuisine for as little as $3 to $5 USD per meal. These meals are not only economical but also provide a glimpse into the local culture and culinary traditions. For travelers preferring a more conventional dining experience, mid-range restaurants serve a variety of local and international dishes, with meals priced around $10 to $15 USD. Upscale dining options in major cities or tourist areas offer gourmet experiences, with prices upwards of $25 USD per meal. Don't forget to budget for beverages, snacks, and the occasional treat, like Nicaragua's famous rum or locally-grown coffee.
- **Transportation**: Getting around Nicaragua can be as cheap or as expensive as you make it. The most economical mode of transport is the public bus system, with fares usually under $1 USD, ideal for short distances and experiencing local life. For longer distances, 'chicken buses' (converted school buses) are a staple of Nicaraguan travel, costing only a few dollars for cross-country journeys. Taxis and private drivers offer more convenience and comfort, with fares depending on distance and your negotiation skills – short rides within cities can cost around $5 USD, while longer journeys might be upwards of $20 USD. Renting a car provides the greatest flexibility, with daily rental rates starting from $30 to $40 USD, not including fuel.
- **Activities**: The cost of activities in Nicaragua will vary based on your interests. Many natural attractions, like beaches or hiking in certain areas, are free to enjoy. However, for guided tours,

adventure sports, or cultural experiences, prices can vary. For example, a guided tour of a colonial city like Granada or León might cost between $20 and $30 USD, while adventure activities like volcano boarding or zip-lining can range from $30 to $100 USD. More specialized experiences, such as private guided treks, deep-sea fishing, or scuba diving, can be more expensive.

When planning your budget, it's also wise to set aside a contingency fund for unexpected expenses, souvenirs, or spontaneous adventures that may arise. Remember, while it's important to stick to a budget, allowing some flexibility can enhance your travel experience, giving you the freedom to explore and enjoy Nicaragua's many wonders without undue financial stress.

Weather

Understanding the climate in Nicaragua is essential to planning your trip, as it significantly influences your travel experience. Nicaragua typically experiences two main seasons: the dry season and the rainy season. The dry season, running from November to April, is generally considered the best time to visit. During these months, you'll enjoy sunny days with minimal rainfall, making it ideal for exploring the outdoors, whether it's city walking tours or hiking in the countryside. However, be aware that the dry season can also bring dusty conditions, especially on unpaved roads or rural areas. Walking around in sandals or open shoes might leave you with dirty feet, so packing a pair of closed shoes is advisable.

On the other hand, the rainy season, from May to October, transforms the landscape into a lush, green environment. While this season offers its own beauty, it also comes with challenges. Rain, often heavy and short-lived, typically occurs in the afternoon or evening. This can lead to muddy conditions on unpaved roads and trails, so waterproof footwear and rain gear become essential items in your packing list. The rainy season also tends to be less crowded, offering a more serene experience at popular tourist spots.

When it comes to mosquitoes, they are present year-round, but their numbers peak during the rainy season due to the increase in standing water, which serves as ideal breeding grounds. The best time to avoid mosquitoes is during the dry season, especially in the early months like December and January. Regardless of when you visit, it's wise to carry mosquito repellent and wear long-sleeved clothing, especially in the evenings or when visiting rural or forested areas.

Each season in Nicaragua has its own charm and challenges. By understanding these weather patterns and planning accordingly, you can choose the ideal time for your visit, ensuring that your experience in this diverse country is both enjoyable and comfortable.

What to Pack

- **Clothing**: Pack light, breathable clothing suitable for warm, tropical weather. Include a mix of short-sleeved shirts, shorts, and a couple of long-sleeved shirts and pants for protection against the sun and mosquitoes. For beach destinations, don't forget swimsuits and a cover-up. If your itinerary includes hiking, especially in the cooler, mountainous regions, bring along a light jacket or sweater.
- **Footwear**: Comfortable walking shoes are a must for city explorations and light hiking. For beach visits and casual wear, sandals or flip-flops are convenient. If you plan on more rigorous hiking,

consider packing a pair of sturdy hiking boots.
- **Rain Gear**: During the rainy season, a lightweight, waterproof jacket or poncho will keep you dry during sudden downpours. Even outside the rainy season, it's a good idea to pack some form of rain protection, as occasional showers can occur.
- **Sun Protection**: Nicaragua's sun can be intense. Bring a high-SPF sunscreen, sunglasses, and a wide-brimmed hat to protect yourself from UV rays.
- **Mosquito Repellent**: Essential for evenings and in rural or forested areas, mosquito repellent will help protect you from bites and potential mosquito-borne diseases.
- **Water Bottle**: Staying hydrated is key in the tropical climate. A reusable water bottle is environmentally friendly and can be refilled at your accommodation or purchased water stations.
- **Basic First Aid Kit**: Include basics like band-aids, antiseptic wipes, and any personal medications. It's also wise to bring along remedies for common travel ailments like upset stomachs or headaches.
- **Daypack**: A lightweight, comfortable backpack is useful for day trips, hikes, or beach outings, allowing you to carry essentials like water, snacks, and your camera.
- **Cultural Considerations**: While Nicaraguans are generally casual in dress, it's respectful to cover up more when visiting religious sites or traditional communities. Including a few modest clothing options in your packing list is advisable.
- **Tech Gear**: Don't forget chargers for your electronic devices, and consider a portable charger for long days out. A camera or smartphone for photos and a travel adapter if needed for your devices are also essential.

Where to Stay

Nicaragua's array of accommodation options caters to every traveler's needs, preferences, and budget, ensuring that you'll find the perfect place to stay. Whether you're seeking the luxury of a high-end hotel, the cozy charm of a boutique guesthouse, or the budget-friendly simplicity of a hostel, Nicaragua has it all. For those on a tight budget, hostels and budget hotels are abundant, offering basic yet comfortable lodgings often with communal areas to socialize and share travel tips. Prices for these accommodations can be incredibly affordable, making them ideal for backpackers or solo travelers.

Mid-range travelers have a wealth of options, from charming B&Bs to locally-owned guesthouses. These often provide a more authentic Nicaraguan experience, combining comfort with a taste of local hospitality. Many of these establishments are strategically located, offering easy access to popular tourist attractions and local dining options.

For those looking for a touch of luxury, Nicaragua's upscale hotels and beachfront resorts offer a range of amenities, including pools, spas, fine dining, and exceptional service. While these are at the higher end of the budget spectrum, they often provide a level of comfort and convenience that can be worth the extra expense, especially for those looking to relax and indulge.

In Nicaragua's more remote or rural areas, eco-lodges and nature-oriented accommodations provide unique experiences, allowing you to immerse yourself in the country's natural beauty. These can range from rustic to luxury, but all offer a closer connection to the natural environment.

When choosing where to stay, consider not just your budget but also the type of experience you want to have. Whether it's waking up to the sound of the ocean in a beachfront cabana, enjoying the bustling atmosphere of a city center hotel, or retreating to a quiet eco-lodge in the rainforest, Nicaragua offers accommodations to suit every preference and budget. By selecting the right accommodation for your needs, you can enhance your overall experience and enjoyment of this diverse and captivating country.

Two Personal Recommendations:

- El Guayacan Retreat: This 5-star hotel in Valle la Laguna offers impressive amenities like an outdoor swimming pool, free parking, a garden, and a terrace. It's more on the luxurious side and has breathtaking views.
- https://www.elguayacanretreat.com/
- Hotel La Polvora: Known for its excellent service and comfortable ambiance. A great choice for travelers seeking a blend of modern amenities and local charm.
- https://www.hotellapolvora.com/

Transportation

Navigating the transportation options in Nicaragua is an integral part of the adventure, offering a genuine immersion into the local culture. Public buses, known locally as 'chicken buses,' are the most common and cost-effective way to travel. These colorful, often crowded buses are a staple of Nicaraguan life, connecting cities and rural areas alike. Fares are exceptionally low, often less than a dollar, making them a budget-friendly option for longer journeys. However, they can be quite slow and sometimes uncomfortable, so patience and a sense of adventure are key.

For a more comfortable and flexible option, consider taxis or private transfers. Taxis are readily available in cities and tourist areas, and while they are more expensive than buses, they remain reasonably priced. Always agree on a fare before setting off, as most taxis do not have meters. For longer distances or day trips, hiring a private driver can be a convenient and efficient way to travel, allowing you to explore at your own pace.

Renting a car gives you the ultimate freedom to explore Nicaragua on your terms. It's particularly useful if you plan to visit more remote areas or prefer not to be tied to bus schedules. Rental costs vary but typically start at around $30-40 per day. Keep in mind that while Nicaragua's main roads are generally in good condition, secondary roads can be challenging, especially in the rainy season. Always carry a map or GPS device, as road signage can be limited.

Another popular option, especially in tourist destinations like Granada or San Juan del Sur, is to rent bicycles or scooters. These provide a fun and flexible way to explore local areas and are particularly enjoyable in Nicaragua's pleasant climate.

Whatever mode of transportation you choose, embracing the local way of getting around is a fantastic opportunity to connect with the country and its people. It's a chance to step out of your comfort zone and experience the rhythms of everyday Nicaraguan life. With a bit of planning and an open mind, navigating Nicaragua's transport system can be a rewarding and enriching part of your travel experience.

How Long Should I Stay

Determining the ideal length for your stay in Nicaragua is key to ensuring a fulfilling travel experience. Whether you have a week, a fortnight, or a month at your disposal, strategic planning can help you make the most of your time. For a shorter stay of about a week, focus on one or two regions to avoid feeling rushed. For instance, you could spend a few days exploring the colonial charm of Granada and its surrounding natural attractions like the Mombacho Volcano and Laguna de Apoyo, then head to the beaches of San Juan del Sur for some relaxation and surf. This allows you to experience both the cultural and natural sides of Nicaragua without overextending yourself.

If you have two weeks, you can afford to explore a wider range of experiences. Add destinations like the enchanting city of León, known for its rich history and vibrant street art, and perhaps venture to the Corn Islands for pristine Caribbean beaches. With two weeks, you can balance your time between urban exploration, cultural immersion, and natural escapades.

For those fortunate enough to spend a month or more in Nicaragua, the possibilities are vast. You can delve deeper into each region, uncovering hidden gems and experiencing the local way of life. Take your time to wander through the markets of Masaya, hike the cloud forests of Matagalpa, or even enroll in a Spanish language course to enhance your cultural immersion.

No matter the length of your stay, it's important to consider travel times between destinations. Nicaragua's diverse geography means that traveling from one region to another can take longer than expected, especially if relying on public transportation. Allowing for these travel days will ensure you don't feel hurried and can fully appreciate each unique part of Nicaragua. By thoughtfully allocating your time, you can leave with a rich tapestry of experiences, from the buzz of city life to the tranquility of nature, each weaving into your memory a vivid picture of Nicaragua.

3

Getting Settled Once You Arrive

U pon arriving in Nicaragua, the journey to getting comfortably settled in your new surroundings begins. This chapter is dedicated to helping you transition smoothly from the moment you step off the plane to feeling at home in your chosen accommodation.

Transport to Your Hotel/Airbnb

Upon your arrival in Nicaragua, getting to your hotel or Airbnb can be a seamless experience with a variety of transportation options available. Here are the most common methods:

GETTING SETTLED ONCE YOU ARRIVE

- Hotel Shuttles: Many hotels, especially those near major tourist destinations or the airport, offer shuttle services. It's advisable to check with your hotel in advance and book a shuttle, if available. This option provides convenience and peace of mind, especially for first-time visitors.
- Taxis: Taxis are readily available at the airport and are a reliable way to reach your destination. They're typically parked outside the arrivals area. It's recommended to use official airport taxis for safety and to agree on the fare before you start your journey, as most taxis don't use meters.
- Public Buses: For those looking for a more economical or authentic travel experience, public buses are an option. They are less comfortable and take longer than taxis or shuttles but offer a glimpse into local life. Be mindful of your luggage and personal belongings, as these buses can get crowded.
- Car Rentals: Renting a car right from the airport is another option, offering flexibility throughout your stay. This is ideal for travelers planning to visit multiple destinations or those who prefer not to rely on public transport. Ensure you're comfortable with local driving conditions and have the necessary documentation.
- Private Transfers: Private transfer services can be booked in advance and offer a personalized experience. This option is more expensive than public transport but offers convenience, especially for groups or families with significant luggage.

Each of these options has its advantages, depending on your budget, comfort level, and travel preferences. Whether you prefer the convenience of a hotel shuttle, the adventure of a public bus, or the independence of a rental car, navigating from the airport to your accommodation can be a smooth start to your Nicaraguan adventure.

What to Expect to See Driving From the Airport to Your Hotel/Airbnb

As you embark on your journey from the airport to your hotel or Airbnb in Nicaragua, you'll be immediately immersed in the vivid tableau of Nicaraguan life, reflecting a 'work-to-eat' culture deeply ingrained in its society. The streets here are bustling with activity, embodying the relentless industriousness of the local populace. You'll see people of all ages, constantly on the move, with many walking alongside the roads or engaged in various street-side businesses. A striking aspect of this landscape is the family dynamic in work; it's not uncommon to witness children working alongside their parents, contributing to family-run ventures or performing small, helpful tasks. This collective effort in livelihoods is a poignant reflection of the community's ethos.

As your vehicle stops at traffic lights, particularly in urban areas, you're likely to encounter street performers. These performers, often youngsters, bring a lively, colorful energy to the urban environment. Their impromptu shows – ranging from music to juggling acts – are a creative expression of seeking livelihood, marking a unique aspect of street life in Nicaragua. Amidst this vibrancy, you'll also notice a more sobering reality – the presence of litter on the streets. While it's a part of life in certain areas and can be initially startling, it underscores the ongoing challenges and gradual progress in environmental management in the country.

This initial drive offers more than just a route to your destination; it's a firsthand glimpse into the real, unvarnished daily life of Nicaragua. Observing these scenes, with an understanding and respectful mindset, enriches your travel experience, offering a deeper insight into the resilience and spirit of the Nicaraguan people.

Managing Jet Lag

When you arrive in Nicaragua, especially if coming from a distant time zone, you might face the common traveler's challenge of jet lag. Adjusting to the local time zone as quickly as possible is key to making the most of your trip. Here are some strategies to help you manage and overcome jet lag efficiently:

- **Adapt to Local Time Immediately**: As soon as you land, try to sync your activities with the local time. If you arrive during the day, resist the urge to sleep immediately, even if it's night in your home time zone. This helps reset your internal clock faster.
- **Stay Hydrated**: Long flights and different climates can dehydrate you, exacerbating the effects of jet lag. Drink plenty of water before, during, and after your flight. Avoiding excessive alcohol and caffeine can also help, as they can disrupt sleep patterns and lead to dehydration.
- **Seek Sunlight**: Exposure to natural light is a powerful tool for resetting your body clock. Spend time outdoors during daylight hours, especially in the morning. Sunlight signals to your body that it's time to be awake and active, aiding the adjustment process.
- **Take Short Naps**: If you're feeling overwhelmingly sleepy during the day, opt for short naps (20-30 minutes) rather than long sleep periods. This can provide a refreshing boost without throwing off your sleep schedule for the night.
- **Gradual Adjustment Before Travel**: If possible, start adjusting your sleep schedule a few days before your trip. Shift your sleeping and eating times closer to the schedule of your destination. This gradual change can lessen the impact upon arrival.
- **Light Exercise**: Engaging in light exercise, like walking or stretching, can invigorate your body and improve your mood and energy levels.

By implementing these tactics, you can minimize the disruptive effects of jet lag and more quickly adapt to Nicaragua's time zone, ensuring you're ready to explore and enjoy your new surroundings from the get-go. Remember, patience and self-care are important as your body adjusts to the new environment.

Supermarket/Non-Restaurant Food Options

One of the most immersive ways to experience the culture of Nicaragua is through its supermarkets and local markets. These places are not just about buying food; they offer a glimpse into the everyday life of Nicaraguans and their culinary traditions.

- **Local Supermarkets**: In Nicaraguan supermarkets, you'll find a wide range of products, including both local and international goods. They are excellent for stocking up on essentials like bottled water, snacks, and basic cooking ingredients. Supermarkets often have a section dedicated to fresh produce, where you can find a variety of fruits and vegetables, many of which are locally grown and incredibly fresh.
- **Markets**: For a more authentic experience, visit the local markets. Markets like Mercado Central in Managua or Mercado Municipal in Granada are bustling hubs of activity where locals shop for their daily needs. Here, you'll find an array of fresh produce, meats, spices, and local delicacies. The colors, smells, and sounds of these markets provide a sensory feast and a deeper insight into Nicaraguan cuisine and lifestyle.
- **Local Snacks and Ingredients**: These markets are also great places to discover local snacks and ingredients unique to Nicaraguan cuisine. Look out for items like queso fresco (a local cheese), plantains, and various beans. You might also find exotic fruits like jocote, nancite, or pitahaya, which are worth trying.

- **Cooking Local Dishes**: If your accommodation includes kitchen facilities, cooking a local dish can be a rewarding experience. Simple and popular Nicaraguan dishes like gallo pinto (a rice and beans dish) or indio viejo (a traditional cornmeal dish) can be easily prepared with ingredients from these markets.
- **Interaction with Locals:** Shopping at these markets also offers an opportunity to interact with local vendors. Nicaraguans are generally friendly and engaging, and such interactions can be enriching, offering insights into local customs and recommendations on the best produce or ingredients to buy.

Exploring these supermarkets and markets not only satisfies your culinary needs but also connects you more deeply with the Nicaraguan way of life. It's an experience that goes beyond mere sightseeing, allowing you to engage with the community and appreciate the rich tapestry of local flavors and customs.

Wildlife to Expect

Nicaragua's diverse ecosystems are a haven for wildlife enthusiasts, boasting a rich array of animal species that thrive in its varied habitats. Whether you're trekking through the lush rainforests or exploring the countryside, here's what you can expect in terms of wildlife sightings:

- **Birds**: Nicaragua is a paradise for birdwatchers, with its forests and lakes hosting an impressive variety of bird species. Keep an eye out for the resplendent quetzal, known for its vibrant colors and long tail feathers. Additionally, you might spot hummingbirds, toucans, and parrots, especially in the more tropical regions.
- **Monkeys**: The forests of Nicaragua are home to several species of monkeys. Howler monkeys are perhaps the most notable, known for their distinctive loud calls that can be heard miles away. You

might also see capuchin monkeys, which are often spotted in groups, playfully moving through the treetops.
- **Sloths**: If you're lucky, you may encounter sloths, particularly in the more forested areas. These slow-moving creatures are often found high in the trees, and spotting them requires a keen eye. They are a unique and fascinating sight, embodying the tranquil pace of life in the Nicaraguan forests.
- **Respect for Wildlife**: While encountering these animals can be exciting, it's important to respect their natural habitat. Maintain a safe distance, avoid feeding or touching them, and use quiet voices to prevent disturbing them. Observing these guidelines ensures that the wildlife remains safe and undisturbed, allowing future visitors to enjoy similar experiences.

Experiencing Nicaragua's wildlife is one of the highlights of visiting this biodiverse country. It offers a chance to connect with nature and witness the beauty of these animals in their natural environment, adding a memorable and enriching aspect to your Nicaraguan adventure.

Sea Life to Expect

Nicaragua's coastal waters and the idyllic Corn Islands are a treasure trove for lovers of marine life. The Caribbean and Pacific coasts of Nicaragua offer distinct and vibrant underwater ecosystems that are a delight to explore.

- **Coral Reefs**: The Corn Islands, in particular, are renowned for their stunning coral reefs. These vibrant ecosystems are bustling with life and color. Snorkeling or diving around these reefs, you'll be treated to a spectacular display of coral formations, providing a habitat for a myriad of marine creatures.
- **Tropical Fish**: The warm waters around Nicaragua are home to a

dazzling variety of tropical fish. Expect to see schools of brightly colored fish, such as parrotfish, angelfish, and butterflyfish, weaving through the corals. The diversity of species and colors is a visual feast and makes for an unforgettable underwater experience.
- **Sea Turtles**: Nicaragua's coasts are also a habitat for several species of sea turtles. With some luck, you may encounter these graceful creatures while snorkeling or diving. They are often seen gliding serenely through the water or feeding on seagrass and algae.
- **Responsible Observation**: When exploring Nicaragua's marine environments, it's important to be a responsible observer. Avoid touching the coral or disturbing the wildlife, as human interaction can have a negative impact on these delicate ecosystems. Always follow the guidelines provided by your tour operator or guide.

Experiencing sea life in Nicaragua is a chance to witness the beauty and complexity of the ocean's ecosystems. Whether you're snorkeling just off the beach or diving in deeper waters, the underwater world here will leave you with a profound appreciation for the ocean's wonders and the need to protect them.

Sounds and Noises

In Nicaragua, the sounds and noises around you are as much a part of the experience as the sights and activities. The country's lively essence is captured in its diverse soundscape, which varies from urban areas to the tranquility of nature. In rural regions, your mornings and evenings are often serenaded by nature's melodies: a chorus of tropical birds greeting the dawn and a symphony of crickets and frogs as night falls. These natural sounds provide a peaceful and immersive backdrop to your stay in the countryside.

In contrast, the urban environments buzz with the vibrant energy of city life. The streets in cities are alive with the constant hum of traffic, the lively chatter of pedestrians, and the energetic bustle of markets, where vendors energetically advertise their wares and bargain with customers. An integral part of this urban soundscape is the rhythmic beats of Nicaraguan music, echoing through the streets. The sounds of marimba, guitars, and local festivals are common, adding a cultural richness to the atmosphere.

A distinctive and ubiquitous sound in Nicaragua is the honking of the chicken buses. These colorful, often crowded buses are not just a means of transport but a cultural icon, known for their vibrant decorations and the characteristic sound of their horns echoing through the streets; sometimes very early in the morning. In addition to these, the everyday sounds of life – the laughter of children playing, neighbors engaging in conversation, dogs barking in the distance – all contribute to the authentic and vibrant sound tapestry of Nicaragua. These everyday noises, though simple, form a connection to the daily lives of the local people, adding authenticity to your Nicaraguan adventure.

4

The Foods of Nicaragua

Nicaragua's culinary landscape is as rich and diverse as its culture, offering a range of flavors and dishes that are a must-try for any visitor. This chapter delves into the most iconic and delicious Nicaraguan foods, explaining what they are, their cultural significance, and where to find the best versions in the country.

Gallo Pinto

Gallo Pinto is a dish that holds a special place in the heart of Nicaraguan cuisine, often hailed as the national dish. At its core, Gallo Pinto is a humble yet flavorful combination of rice and beans, two staples of

Central American cooking. The beans and rice are typically pre-cooked and then fried together, allowing the flavors to meld. Onions, bell peppers, and a subtle blend of spices like garlic and cumin are often added to enhance the taste.

Traditionally served as a breakfast dish, Gallo Pinto provides a hearty and nourishing start to the day. It's common to find it accompanied by eggs, which can be cooked to preference, be it scrambled, fried, or boiled. A side of fresh cheese, known locally as 'queso fresco', and fried plantains add a delightful balance of salty and sweet to the meal, creating a symphony of flavors in every bite.

The beauty of Gallo Pinto lies in its simplicity and versatility. It is a dish that transcends social and economic boundaries, enjoyed equally by people from all walks of life. You can find it almost everywhere in Nicaragua, from the most unassuming roadside stands to upscale restaurants in major cities. Each cook adds their personal touch to it, making every version of Gallo Pinto slightly unique.

Not only is Gallo Pinto a culinary staple, but it also serves as a cultural symbol, representing the blending of indigenous and Spanish influences that define much of Nicaraguan culture. Sampling Gallo Pinto is more than just enjoying a meal; it's an experience of the nation's heritage and a must-try for anyone seeking to understand and appreciate the true essence of Nicaraguan cuisine.

Nacatamales

Nacatamales are much more than just a dish in Nicaragua; they are a cherished tradition, often reserved for special occasions and family gatherings. This beloved dish consists of a rich, seasoned corn dough that is generously filled with a mixture of meat (usually pork or chicken), rice, potatoes, and a variety of vegetables like tomatoes, onions, and bell peppers. The ingredients are carefully wrapped in plantain leaves, which impart a subtle earthy flavor during the steaming process.

The preparation of Nacatamales is a labor of love and a communal activity. It's common for families to come together to make them in large batches, sharing the workload and the joy of cooking. The process is time-consuming, involving the careful assembly of each tamale, but the result is a flavorful and satisfying meal that embodies the spirit of Nicaraguan hospitality.

Nacatamales are typically enjoyed during breakfast or as a main meal, savored for their hearty and comforting qualities. The dish is a staple during festive occasions, holidays, and on weekends, when families have the time to gather and enjoy the meal together.

For visitors to Nicaragua, the best Nacatamales are often found at local markets, where they're made fresh daily. Alternatively, asking locals for their recommendations can lead you to hidden gems where you can experience authentic and homemade Nacatamales. Whether you're trying them from a market stall or at a family-run eatery, tasting Nacatamales is a foray into the heart of Nicaraguan culinary tradition, offering a unique insight into the country's culture and communal values.

Indio Viejo

Indio Viejo, translating to "Old Indian," is a dish steeped in history, its flavors and ingredients telling a story of Nicaragua's rich indigenous and colonial heritage. This hearty stew is a staple of traditional Nicaraguan cuisine, beloved for its depth of flavor and comforting qualities.

The base of Indio Viejo is a thick, savory mixture made from masa de maíz, or corn dough, which gives the stew its distinctive texture. To this base, shredded meat – typically beef or chicken – is added, along with a medley of local vegetables. Common additions include onions, bell peppers, and tomatoes, which are sautéed with the meat to enhance their natural sweetness. The stew is seasoned with a blend of Nicaraguan spices, often including garlic, achiote (annatto), and sour orange juice, which contribute to its rich, complex flavor profile.

Indio Viejo is more than just a dish; it is a culinary journey through time, with each ingredient and method of preparation echoing Nicaragua's past. The use of corn dough harks back to the staple grain of the indigenous populations, while the cooking techniques and added spices reflect the influence of Spanish colonial cuisine.

For those seeking an authentic taste of Nicaraguan culture, Indio Viejo is a must-try dish. It is commonly found in traditional Nicaraguan restaurants, where it is prepared following age-old recipes. Eating Indio Viejo is not only a delight for the taste buds but also an opportunity to connect with the history and traditions of Nicaragua, making it a unique and enriching culinary experience.

Vigorón

Vigorón is a quintessential Nicaraguan street food, celebrated for its bold flavors and satisfying textures. A classic example of Nicaraguan culinary ingenuity, this dish combines simple ingredients to create a harmonious and delectable meal.

At the heart of Vigorón is boiled yuca, also known as cassava, which forms a starchy and soft base. The yuca is topped with crunchy chicharrón, or fried pork skin, adding a rich and savory element to the dish. The combination of the tender yuca and the crispy chicharrón creates a delightful contrast both in texture and flavor.

Complementing these components is a tangy cabbage salad, typically made with shredded cabbage, tomatoes, onions, and a zesty vinegar or lime dressing. This salad adds a fresh and acidic note to the dish, balancing the richness of the chicharrón and the heartiness of the yuca.

Traditionally, Vigorón is served on a plantain leaf, which not only acts as an eco-friendly plate but also imparts a subtle earthy aroma to the dish. This presentation is a nod to Nicaragua's commitment to using natural and locally available materials.

Vigorón holds a special place in the city of Granada, where it is particularly popular. The streets and markets around Granada's central park are dotted with vendors offering this iconic dish. These stalls, with their vibrant atmosphere and the enticing aroma of freshly prepared Vigorón, are a must-visit for anyone seeking to experience the authentic street food culture of Nicaragua.

Eating Vigorón is not just a culinary delight but also an experience in itself, offering a taste of the local lifestyle and a glimpse into the simplicity and richness of Nicaraguan cuisine. It's a dish that encapsulates the spirit of Nicaraguan street food – unpretentious, flavorful, and deeply satisfying.

Quesillo

Quesillo is a beloved Nicaraguan snack, known for its simplicity and delightful flavors. It's a testament to how a few basic ingredients can come together to create something truly enjoyable. A quesillo consists of a soft corn tortilla filled with a generous amount of soft, melty cheese. The cheese used is typically a local variety, which has a mild yet distinct flavor and a stringy, gooey texture when melted.

To the cheese-filled tortilla, finely chopped onions are added, providing a sharp, piquant contrast to the richness of the cheese. The quesillo is then liberally drizzled with sour cream, adding a creamy and tangy element that ties all the flavors together beautifully.

What makes quesillo particularly appealing is its portability. It is often served wrapped in a plastic bag or a plantain leaf, making it an easy snack to enjoy on the go. This no-fuss approach to serving and eating adds to its charm and popularity as street food.

The town of Nagarote, situated on the shores of Lake Managua, is renowned for its quesillos and is often referred to as the birthplace of this delicious snack. Here, roadside stands and small eateries specialize in quesillos, each boasting their own family recipe passed down through generations. These quesillos are acclaimed for their authenticity and flavor, drawing food enthusiasts from all over the country.

A visit to Nagarote, with its rows of quesillo stands, offers a unique culinary experience. Here, you can savor this humble yet flavorful snack, often accompanied by a refreshing, chilled drink, and immerse yourself in a quintessential aspect of Nicaraguan street food culture. The quesillo, with its straightforward yet satisfying taste, is a must-try for anyone looking to experience the essence of Nicaragua's snack cuisine.

Rondón

Rondón is a distinctive and flavorful stew that embodies the culinary traditions of Nicaragua's Caribbean coast. This unique dish is a celebration of the region's abundant seafood and tropical ingredients, creating a taste experience that is both rich and satisfying.

The base of Rondón is a creamy, aromatic coconut milk broth, which sets the stage for the rest of the ingredients. The stew typically features a variety of fish or seafood, depending on what is freshly available or the 'catch of the day'. This could include snapper, conch, shrimp, or even lobster, each bringing its own distinct flavor and texture to the dish.

Accompanying the seafood are hearty, starchy vegetables that are staples in Nicaraguan cuisine. Plantains and yuca (cassava) are commonly used, adding a subtle sweetness and a satisfying bite to the stew. Other vegetables like bell peppers, onions, and carrots are also often included, contributing to the depth of flavor and nutritional value of the dish.

What makes Rondón particularly special is its variability - no two pots of Rondón are exactly the same. Each chef brings their personal touch to the recipe, influenced by their preferences and the ingredients available to them. This means that every time you have Rondón, you're likely to experience a slightly different, but always delightful, flavor profile.

Rondón is more than just a meal; it's a culinary journey that offers a glimpse into the diverse cultural influences and natural bounty of Nicaragua's Caribbean coast. When visiting this region, indulging in a bowl of Rondón is a must. It's an opportunity to savor a dish that is deeply rooted in the local culture, showcasing the creativity and resourcefulness of Nicaraguan coastal cuisine.

Maduros

Maduros, a beloved side dish in Nicaraguan cuisine, are sweet, ripe plantains that are fried to perfection. This simple yet delicious dish highlights the natural sweetness of plantains, a staple ingredient in many Central American countries.

The preparation of Maduros involves selecting ripe plantains that have turned deep yellow with black spots, indicating their high sugar content. These plantains are sliced and then fried in oil until they achieve a golden-brown color. The frying process caramelizes the natural sugars in the plantains, resulting in a delightful outer crispness and a soft, sweet interior.

Maduros serve as a perfect counterpoint to savory dishes, offering a balance of flavors on the plate. Their natural sweetness complements a wide range of Nicaraguan specialties, from hearty meats to flavorful rice and bean dishes. This versatility makes Maduros a popular and ubiquitous side dish in Nicaraguan cuisine.

You can find Maduros in nearly every Nicaraguan restaurant, from local eateries to more upscale dining establishments. They are often served as part of a traditional meal, alongside dishes like Gallo Pinto or grilled meats. In addition to their delicious taste, Maduros add a vibrant splash of color to the meal, making them as visually appealing as they are tasty.

For anyone exploring the culinary landscape of Nicaragua, trying Maduros is a must. This simple dish not only offers a taste of the local flavor but also showcases the importance of plantains in the Nicaraguan diet. Whether enjoyed on their own or as a complement to a larger meal, Maduros are a delightful and essential part of the Nicaraguan dining experience.

Tres Leches Cake

In the realm of Nicaraguan desserts, Tres Leches Cake stands out as an indulgent and beloved treat. Its name, translating to "Three Milks Cake," aptly describes this delicacy that is both sumptuous and comforting. Tres Leches is a light and airy sponge cake that forms the base for a luxurious soaking of three different types of milk: evaporated milk, condensed milk, and heavy cream or whole milk. This combination imbues the cake with a richness and moistness that is unparalleled, creating a dessert that is both satisfying and irresistible.

The process of soaking ensures that every bite is infused with creamy sweetness, but the cake surprisingly retains a light texture, preventing it from becoming overly dense. It's often topped with a light meringue or whipped cream frosting, adding a final touch of decadence. In some variations, a sprinkle of cinnamon or a garnish of fresh fruit is added to balance the richness.

Tres Leches Cake holds a special place in Nicaraguan celebrations and gatherings, symbolizing festivity and indulgence. Its popularity means that it can be found in most Nicaraguan bakeries and restaurants, each offering their own version of this classic dessert.

For visitors with a sweet tooth, trying Tres Leches Cake is a culinary delight not to be missed. It not only offers a taste of Nicaraguan dessert culture but also provides a perfect end to a traditional Nicaraguan meal.

The experience of savoring this moist, milky cake is a delightful journey through texture and flavor, making it a must-try dessert in Nicaragua.

Each of these dishes offers a taste of Nicaragua's rich culinary heritage, blending indigenous, Spanish, and Creole influences. Exploring these flavors is not just about satisfying your taste buds; it's a journey through the history and culture of this vibrant country.

5

Best Hikes

Nicaragua, with its dramatic landscapes and untouched natural beauty, offers some of the most rewarding hiking experiences in Central America. Whether you're an experienced hiker looking for a challenging adventure or a casual walker seeking scenic trails, the country's diverse terrain has something for everyone. In this chapter, we'll explore some of the best hikes in Nicaragua, providing insights into each trail's unique features, difficulty level, access information, and essential tips to make your hiking experience both enjoyable and safe.

Mombacho Volcano

Mombacho Volcano, a dormant stratovolcano near the city of Granada, is a must-visit for hiking enthusiasts exploring Nicaragua. Offering an array of trails that cater to different skill levels, Mombacho is not only a hiking destination but also a journey into a rich ecological haven.

- **The Crater Trail**: The most accessible and popular trail on Mombacho is the Crater Trail, a 1.5 km loop that is relatively easy and suitable for most hikers, including families. This trail encircles one of the volcano's craters and is unique for its cloud forest environment. As you walk through the misty forest, you are enveloped in a lush landscape, home to a variety of orchids, ferns, and mosses. The trail offers several viewpoints, providing breathtaking vistas of Lake Nicaragua, the city of Granada, and the surrounding countryside. The cloud forest's cool, moist conditions make for a refreshing hiking experience.
- **El Puma Trail**: For those seeking a more challenging hike, the El Puma Trail presents a higher difficulty level. This trail is longer and more strenuous, winding through less frequented parts of the volcano. It's an ideal choice for serious hikers and nature enthusiasts. As you ascend along this trail, you'll experience a change in ecosystems and a chance to observe a greater diversity of flora and fauna. The El Puma Trail is a testament to Mombacho's rich biodiversity, offering opportunities to spot rare birds, butterflies, and possibly even howler monkeys.
- **Facilities and Guides**: At the base of Mombacho, near the biological station, ample parking is available for visitors. Here, you can also find guides for hire. While the Crater Trail can be navigated without a guide, hiring one for the El Puma Trail can enrich your experience, offering insights into the volcano's ecosystem and ensuring a safe journey. Additionally, the biological

station serves as an educational resource, providing information about the volcano and its surrounding natural environment.

Whether you choose the leisurely Crater Trail with its stunning views and unique cloud forest or the more adventurous El Puma Trail, hiking Mombacho Volcano is an experience that combines physical activity with the awe-inspiring beauty of Nicaragua's natural landscapes. It's an opportunity to immerse yourself in the tranquility of nature while exploring one of the country's most iconic landmarks.

Masaya Volcano

Hiking the Masaya Volcano offers a truly unique and awe-inspiring experience, especially known for its remarkable active lava lake. Situated within the Masaya Volcano National Park, this volcano presents a rare opportunity to witness the raw power of nature up close.

- **The Santiago Crater Trek:** The most captivating trail at Masaya Volcano leads to the Santiago crater, an active vent where you can observe the mesmerizing sight of glowing lava. This trek is an unforgettable experience, particularly striking at night when the lava's glow becomes a fiery spectacle against the dark sky. The trail to the Santiago crater is relatively easy to navigate, making it accessible to a wide range of hikers. The sight of the lava lake, emitting its red and orange hues, is not only a visual wonder but also an intriguing lesson in geology.
- **Trail Difficulty and Safety**: While the physical demands of the trails around Masaya Volcano are generally moderate, the main challenge lies in the volcanic gasses. These gasses can be strong and potentially hazardous, so it is crucial for hikers to be aware of the wind conditions. The park authorities monitor these conditions closely and can advise on the safest times to hike. It's recommended

to visit when the winds are favorable, blowing the gasses away from hiking paths.

- **Visiting at Night:** For those interested in observing the lava at night, guided night tours are available. These tours offer a safe and informative way to experience the volcano after dark, highlighting the dramatic contrast of the glowing lava against the night sky. The cooler evening temperatures also make for a comfortable hiking experience.
- **Preparation and Precautions:** When planning your hike to Masaya Volcano, it's wise to prepare for varying conditions. Bringing water, wearing comfortable hiking shoes, and carrying a light jacket for the evenings are advisable. Additionally, due to the presence of volcanic gasses, carrying a respiratory mask or scarf can be beneficial.
- **Parking:** Overall, parking at Masaya Volcano National Park is user-friendly, adding to the ease and enjoyment of your visit. The close proximity of the parking to key attractions, along with the safety measures in place, ensures a smooth and hassle-free start to your exploration of this magnificent natural wonder.

Hiking to Masaya Volcano is more than just a trek; it's an encounter with one of nature's most fascinating phenomena. The experience of standing at the edge of an active crater, observing the molten heart of the earth, is a powerful reminder of the planet's dynamic and ever-changing nature. It's an adventure that combines physical activity, natural beauty, and geological exploration, making it a must-do for anyone visiting Nicaragua.

Concepción Volcano

For the adventurous and experienced hiker, the climb up Concepción Volcano presents an exhilarating challenge. As one of Nicaragua's highest and most active volcanoes, it offers a hiking experience that is both physically demanding and immensely rewarding.

- **The Hike**: The trail to the summit of Concepción Volcano is known for its steep and rugged terrain. The ascent is a test of endurance, often involving a climb through varying environments, from tropical dry forest at the base to cloud forest as you ascend. The hike can take up to 10 hours for a round trip, depending on your pace and experience. Given its difficulty, this hike is recommended for those with a good level of physical fitness and prior hiking experience.
- **The Summit Experience**: Reaching the summit of Concepción Volcano is an achievement that comes with its own spectacular reward. Hikers are treated to panoramic views of the surrounding landscape, including the stunning vista of Lake Nicaragua and the neighboring Maderas Volcano. On clear days, the view extends as far as the eye can see, providing a truly breathtaking experience.
- **Fees and Regulations**: There is typically an entrance fee to access the trail, which contributes to the conservation and maintenance of the area. The fee is usually payable at a ranger station or visitor center at the base of the volcano. Since Concepción is an active volcano, it's important to check any volcanic activity reports and weather conditions before attempting the hike.
- **Parking**: Parking is available at the base of the volcano, usually near the trailhead or a designated visitor area. The parking facilities are generally basic but adequate for hikers' needs. It's advisable to arrive early to secure a spot, especially during peak hiking seasons.
- **Safety and Preparation**: Due to the challenging nature of this hike, it's crucial to come well-prepared. This includes carrying sufficient water, wearing appropriate hiking gear, and considering the use of hiking poles for additional support. Hiring a local guide is highly

recommended, as they can provide valuable insights into the trail conditions and ensure a safer hiking experience.

Hiking Concepción Volcano is an adventure that promises not just a physical journey but also an unforgettable encounter with the raw beauty of Nicaragua's volcanic landscape. The effort required to reach the summit is amply rewarded with stunning views and a sense of accomplishment that resonates long after the hike is completed.

Cerro Negro Volcano

Cerro Negro, known widely for the thrilling sport of volcano boarding, also presents a unique and memorable hiking experience. This active volcano, with its stark black ash slopes and lunar-like landscape, offers a different kind of adventure for those looking to explore Nicaragua's volcanic terrain.

- **The Hike**: The ascent of Cerro Negro is both steep and exhilarating, yet it is relatively short compared to other volcano hikes in Nicaragua. Typically, the hike to the summit takes about an hour, making it accessible even for those with a moderate fitness level. The path is straightforward but involves walking on loose volcanic gravel, which can be a bit challenging.
- **The Summit and Volcano Boarding**: Once at the top, hikers are rewarded with stunning panoramic views of the surrounding landscapes, including a series of other volcanoes lining the horizon. The unique aspect of Cerro Negro is the opportunity to volcano board down its slopes, an activity that has gained popularity and attracted thrill-seekers from around the world. Sliding down the volcanic ash slopes on a specially designed board is an exhilarating experience and a highlight for many visitors.
- **Fees and Regulations**: There is an entrance fee to access Cerro

Negro, which is used for the conservation and maintenance of the area. Additionally, if you plan to volcano board, there are rental fees for the boards and protective gear. It's advisable to book this experience through a reputable tour operator, which often includes the rental and transportation costs.
- **Parking**: Parking facilities are available at the base of Cerro Negro. The parking area is typically simple and offers enough space for the vehicles of visitors and tour operators. It's a convenient starting point for the hike and the boarding experience.
- **Safety and Preparation**: Despite the relatively easy hike, it's important to come prepared. Wear sturdy shoes for the climb, carry water, and use sun protection, as there is little shade on the volcano. For those planning to board down, protective gear such as jumpsuits, helmets, and goggles is essential and usually provided by tour operators.

Hiking and boarding down Cerro Negro offer a blend of adventure, physical activity, and the chance to witness the unique volcanic landscapes of Nicaragua. It's an experience that combines the thrill of an active adventure with the awe-inspiring beauty of nature, making it a must-do for visitors to the region.

Bosawás Biosphere Reserve

The Bosawás Biosphere Reserve, one of the largest rainforest reserves in Central America, is a haven for hikers and nature enthusiasts. This UNESCO-designated reserve is celebrated for its incredible biodiversity and vast, unspoiled landscapes.

- **Hiking Trails**: Bosawás offers a network of trails that cater to various levels of hiking experience, from easy walks to more challenging treks. These trails meander through dense rainforests, past rivers and waterfalls, and up into cloud forests, offering a diverse range of ecosystems to explore. Hikers have the opportunity to encounter a wide array of wildlife, including exotic birds, monkeys, and possibly even elusive jaguars, though these are rarely seen.

- **Guided Hikes:** Due to the reserve's vastness and the complexity of its ecosystems, hiking in Bosawás is typically done with a guide. Local guides not only ensure safety and help with navigation but also provide valuable insights into the flora, fauna, and ecological significance of the reserve. These guides can usually be arranged through eco-lodges or tour operators in the area.
- **Costs:** There may be a fee to enter the Bosawás Biosphere Reserve, which contributes to its conservation and management. The cost of hiring a guide varies depending on the length and difficulty of the hike. Eco-lodges and tour operators in the region can provide detailed information on the costs associated with guided hikes.
- **Parking**: Parking facilities in Bosawás are limited and are typically associated with eco-lodges or designated entrance points to the reserve. These parking areas are generally basic but sufficient for visitors coming to explore the reserve. It's advisable to confirm parking arrangements with your accommodation or tour operator, especially if you're self-driving to the reserve.
- **Preparation**: When planning a hike in Bosawás, it's crucial to be well-prepared. This includes wearing appropriate footwear, carrying sufficient water, and using insect repellent. Given the reserve's remote location, it's also wise to carry basic first aid supplies.

Hiking in the Bosawás Biosphere Reserve is an immersive experience that connects you with the raw beauty of nature. It's a chance to delve deep into one of the world's most important ecological treasures, offering a unique opportunity to witness the rich biodiversity and pristine landscapes of Nicaragua's rainforest.

Reserva Natural Miraflor

Reserva Natural Miraflor, located in northern Nicaragua, is a hidden gem for nature lovers and hikers alike. Known for its stunning cloud forests and a remarkable variety of orchids, this reserve offers a serene and biodiverse environment ideal for exploration.

- **Diverse Trails**: Miraflor boasts a range of hiking trails suitable for all levels of experience. Whether you're looking for a gentle walk to enjoy the scenic beauty or a more challenging hike to delve deeper into the cloud forest, there's a path for you. These trails wind through varying landscapes, from lush forests to open meadows, providing hikers with a chance to experience the reserve's diverse ecosystems.
- **Flora and Fauna**: The reserve is a haven for biodiversity. It's home to an array of flora, including over 200 species of orchids that thrive in the cloud forest's moist, cool climate. Wildlife enthusiasts may spot a variety of birds, butterflies, and possibly mammals like sloths and armadillos. The rich biodiversity makes every hike in Miraflor a discovery of nature's wonders.
- **Community Engagement**: Miraflor is not just about natural beauty; it's also an opportunity to engage with local communities. Some trails lead to small villages where visitors can learn about the local way of life, traditional agriculture, and even participate in community-based tourism initiatives.
- **Costs**: There is usually a nominal entrance fee to access the trails in

Reserva Natural Miraflor, which contributes to the conservation of the area and the community projects within the reserve. Additional costs may include hiring local guides, which is recommended to enhance your hiking experience and for safety reasons. Local guides offer valuable insights into the area's ecology and help navigate the less marked trails.

- **Parking**: Parking is available at the main entrance of the reserve and near some of the larger eco-lodges. The parking facilities are basic but adequate, ensuring that visitors can securely leave their vehicles as they explore the trails.
- **Preparation**: Due to the reserve's varying altitudes and microclimates, it's advisable to come prepared with suitable clothing. Light rain gear, comfortable hiking boots, and layers are recommended, as the weather can change quickly, especially in the cloud forest areas.

Exploring Reserva Natural Miraflor is an enriching experience, offering a blend of natural beauty, wildlife observation, and cultural encounters. It's a chance to immerse oneself in the tranquility of the Nicaraguan highlands and to appreciate the delicate balance between humans and nature in this unique ecosystem.

Somoto Canyon

Somoto Canyon, located in the northwestern part of Nicaragua, is a spectacular natural wonder that offers an adventurous blend of hiking and water activities. This geological marvel, renowned for its dramatic cliffs and crystal-clear waters, provides an exhilarating experience for both nature enthusiasts and adventure seekers.

- **Hiking the Rim**: The adventure at Somoto Canyon often begins with a hike along its rim. This trek offers stunning views of the canyon from above, allowing hikers to appreciate the grandeur of the towering rock walls and the serenity of the river flowing below. The trail along the rim varies in difficulty, catering to both casual walkers and more experienced hikers. It's an opportunity to witness the canyon's beauty in its entirety and to capture breathtaking photographs.

- **Descending into the Canyon**: The hike eventually leads to a descent into the canyon itself. This transition from the rim to the canyon floor offers a unique perspective of the towering walls and the diverse flora that clings to the rocks.
- **Water Adventure**: Once in the canyon, the experience takes on a new dimension with opportunities for swimming and boating. Visitors can swim in the calm, clear waters, a refreshing reward after the hike. For a different perspective of the canyon, boat tours or tubing are available, allowing you to glide along the river, enveloped by the majestic walls of the canyon. This part of the experience is both relaxing and exhilarating, providing a close-up view of the geological formations and the chance to explore hidden corners of the canyon.
- **Safety and Preparation**: As with any outdoor adventure, safety is paramount. It's advisable to wear appropriate footwear for both the hike and water activities, and to bring along water and sun protection. Life jackets are typically provided for boating or tubing.

Somoto Canyon offers an adventure that is as much about the journey as it is about the destination. The combination of hiking along the rim and then engaging in water activities within the canyon makes for a memorable experience, filled with stunning natural beauty and thrilling moments. This destination is a testament to Nicaragua's diverse and awe-inspiring landscapes, providing an adventure that resonates long after the trip is over.

Each of these hikes offers a unique way to experience Nicaragua's stunning natural landscapes. When planning your hike, consider your fitness level and experience, and always prioritize safety. Hiring local guides can enhance your experience, providing insights into the local environment and culture. With the right preparation, hiking in Nicaragua can be an unforgettable adventure.

Make a Difference with Your Review
Share the Joy of Discovery

"The real voyage of discovery consists not in seeking new landscapes, but in having new eyes." - Marcel Proust, paraphrased

Adventurers and explorers at heart live the fullest lives, filled with stories and memories that last a lifetime. And sometimes, sharing those stories can make all the difference.

Now, here's a thought for you...

Would you light the way for a fellow explorer on their journey through Nicaragua, even if your paths might never cross?

Imagine someone just like you, eager and full of wanderlust, ready to embark on their own Nicaraguan adventure. They're looking for guidance, a signpost to show them the way - and your words could be the very thing they need.

BEST HIKES

Our guide, "Journey Through Nicaragua," is meant to be a compass for all - ensuring that the wonders of Nicaragua are within reach for every traveler. My goal is to open the doors to Nicaragua's treasures for all to enjoy. But to do that, I need to reach the hearts and minds of fellow travelers everywhere.

This is where you come in. Your review is more than just words; it's a beacon for future travelers navigating their choices. So here's my humble request on behalf of a kindred spirit you've never met:

Please take a moment to leave a review for this book.

It doesn't cost a thing, barely takes any time, but your insights could inspire someone's trip of a lifetime. Your shared experience could lead to…

- …another family making unforgettable memories.
- …a couple finding a new favorite getaway.
- …an individual gaining the courage to travel solo.
- …a group of friends experiencing the trip they always talked about.
- …another person's dream journey coming to life.

To spread the joy and offer your guidance, just click the shortened Amazon Review link below to leave your review:

https://qrco.de/jtnica

If the thought of helping an unseen fellow traveler brings a smile to your face, then you truly embody the spirit of discovery. Welcome to our community of globetrotters and story-weavers. You are one of us.

I can't wait to assist you further on your path to more discoveries and adventures in the enchanting lands of Nicaragua. The upcoming chapters are packed with insights and secrets that you won't want to miss.

With heartfelt thanks,
   Elena Carina Mendoza

PS - Remember, sharing your knowledge and experiences not only enriches others but adds to your own journey. If this book has been a valuable guide for you, consider passing it on to another would-be adventurer.

6

Best Beaches

Nicaragua's coastline is dotted with stunning beaches, each offering its own unique charm and array of activities. From secluded coves to vibrant surf spots, the country's beaches are a paradise for sunseekers, surfers, and nature enthusiasts alike. In this chapter, we explore some of the best beaches in Nicaragua, detailing their location, characteristics, recommended activities, parking information, and useful tips for visitors.

Playa Maderas

Playa Maderas, situated a short distance from the popular town of San Juan del Sur, is a haven for surf enthusiasts. Renowned for its consistent waves that cater to both beginners and experienced surfers, this beach is a prime destination for those looking to ride the surf in Nicaragua.

- **The Beach**: The allure of Playa Maderas goes beyond its surf. It boasts picturesque golden sands framed by rugged rocky outcrops, creating a scenic backdrop that's perfect for more than just surfing. The beach's natural beauty makes it an ideal spot for sunbathing, relaxing with a book, or simply soaking in the sun. As the day winds down, Playa Maderas offers some of the most stunning sunsets in the region, with the sky and ocean transforming into a canvas of vibrant colors.
- **Surfing Amenities**: Recognizing its popularity among surfers, Playa Maderas offers a range of surfing amenities. There are several spots along the beach where you can rent surfboards for the day. For those new to surfing or looking to improve their skills, surf lessons are readily available and cater to all levels. The instructors are typically experienced and knowledgeable, providing both group and private lessons.
- **Food and Drink**: Along the beach, visitors will find a selection of laid-back bars and restaurants, adding to the relaxed and friendly atmosphere of Playa Maderas. These establishments serve a variety of food and drinks, from fresh seafood to cold beverages, perfect for refueling after a day in the water.
- **Parking**: For visitors driving to Playa Maderas, there is parking available close to the beach. The parking is typically managed and may require a small fee, which contributes to the upkeep of the area. The convenience of having parking nearby means that visitors can easily transport their surfboards and other beach essentials.

Playa Maderas strikes the perfect balance between a surf hotspot and a serene beach retreat. Whether you're there to catch the perfect wave or to enjoy a peaceful day by the sea, this beach offers a little something for everyone. Its combination of natural beauty, surfing culture, and relaxed ambiance makes it a must-visit spot on Nicaragua's Pacific coast.

Redonda Bay

Redonda Bay is a hidden gem along Nicaragua's Pacific coast, celebrated for its serene beauty and pristine conditions. This secluded beach is a paradise for those seeking tranquility and a chance to connect with nature.

- **Tranquil Waters**: The bay is characterized by its crystal-clear waters, which are calm and inviting, making it an ideal spot for swimming and snorkeling. The clarity of the water provides excellent visibility for exploring the vibrant marine life that inhabits the area. It's a perfect destination for those who enjoy underwater activities in a peaceful setting.
- **Lush Surroundings**: Encircled by lush greenery and tropical vegetation, Redonda Bay feels like a world away from the hustle and bustle of everyday life. The natural surroundings not only provide a beautiful backdrop but also contribute to the sense of seclusion and privacy that makes this beach so special.
- **Access and Hiking**: Reaching Redonda Bay often involves a short hike through scenic trails. This brief trek is part of the beach's charm, offering picturesque views and an opportunity to enjoy the local flora and fauna. The hike is generally suitable for most fitness levels and adds an element of adventure to the journey.
- **Parking Information**: Given its secluded nature, parking options near Redonda Bay are somewhat limited. There are small designated parking areas, but spaces can fill up quickly, especially during peak times. It's advisable to arrive early to secure a parking spot and to enjoy the beach at its quietest.

- **Tips for Visitors**: When visiting Redonda Bay, it's recommended to bring essentials such as water, snacks, and snorkeling gear, as facilities at the beach are minimal. Sun protection is also important due to the open exposure to the sun during the hike and while on the beach.

Redonda Bay's combination of clear waters, serene environment, and lush scenery makes it an ideal destination for those looking to escape to a quieter, more natural beach setting. Whether you're swimming, snorkeling, or simply lounging on the sand, Redonda Bay offers a peaceful retreat and a chance to experience the unspoiled beauty of Nicaragua's coastline.

Playa El Coco

Located south of the bustling town of San Juan del Sur, Playa El Coco stands out as an idyllic retreat, perfect for families and those seeking a more laid-back beach experience. Its tranquil atmosphere and natural beauty make it a favored spot for a peaceful day by the sea.

- **Serene Beach Setting**: Playa El Coco is characterized by its long stretch of soft, golden sand, inviting visitors to stroll, play, or lounge under the sun. The beach's gentle waves are ideal for swimming, especially for families with children. Its relatively calm waters also make it suitable for paddleboarding and kayaking, activities that can be enjoyed by visitors of all ages.
- **Family-Friendly Environment**: The quiet and relaxed vibe of Playa El Coco is especially appealing to families. With plenty of space and a safe, clean environment, it's a fantastic beach for building sandcastles, having a picnic, or simply enjoying time together in a serene setting.

- **Facilities and Amenities**: Though quieter than some of its neighboring beaches, Playa El Coco offers essential facilities, including a few restaurants where visitors can savor fresh seafood and local dishes. The beach is also home to a selection of accommodation options, ranging from cozy guest houses to beachfront rentals, making it convenient for those wishing to stay overnight or longer.
- **Parking Availability**: Ample parking is available at Playa El Coco, ensuring easy access for visitors. The parking areas are conveniently located close to the beach, allowing for easy unloading of beach gear and providing quick access to the sand and sea.
- **Tips for Visitors**: When visiting Playa El Coco, it's advisable to bring along sun protection and any specific beach equipment you may need, such as beach chairs or umbrellas, as rental options might be limited. It's also a good idea to carry cash for purchases at local establishments, as card facilities may not always be available.

Playa El Coco offers a tranquil escape, where the beauty of the Nicaraguan coastline can be enjoyed at a leisurely pace. Its family-friendly atmosphere and picturesque setting make it a charming destination for those looking to unwind and soak up the natural beauty of Nicaragua's beaches.

Las Peñitas

Located conveniently close to the historic city of León, Las Peñitas is a charming beach town that offers a perfect mix of relaxation and local culture. This coastal destination is known for its laid-back vibe and beautiful, expansive sandy beach.

- **Beach Activities**: The long stretch of sand at Las Peñitas is ideal for a variety of beach activities. It is a great spot for swimming, with areas of gentle waves that suit all ages and skill levels. For those interested in surfing, there are several spots along the beach offering good breaks for both beginners and more experienced surfers. Surfboards can often be rented from local shops along the beach.

- **Vibrant Beachfront**: Las Peñitas is not just about the beach; its lively beachfront is dotted with a range of restaurants and bars that add to its appeal. These establishments offer delicious local cuisine, fresh seafood, and the opportunity to enjoy a drink while watching the sunset. The atmosphere here is typically vibrant, with the sound of music and the buzz of conversation adding to the beach town experience.
- **Parking Facilities**: For visitors arriving by car, parking is conveniently available along the beach road. There are ample spaces, ensuring easy access to the beach. The proximity of the parking to the beach means that visitors can easily transport their beach gear and other essentials.
- **Tips for Visitors**: While Las Peñitas is generally quieter than some of Nicaragua's more well-known beaches, it can get lively, especially on weekends and holidays. For a quieter experience, consider visiting on weekdays. Additionally, while the beach town offers basic amenities, it's a good idea to come prepared with essentials like sun protection and enough cash for purchases, as ATM access might be limited.

Las Peñitas strikes a delightful balance between a peaceful beach getaway and a glimpse into Nicaraguan beach life. Its proximity to León makes it a convenient choice for travelers looking to combine a city tour with some time on the coast. Whether you're there to catch some waves, enjoy the local food scene, or just relax on the beach, Las Peñitas offers a welcoming and enjoyable beach experience.

Pearl Cays

The Pearl Cays, a stunning archipelago located off Nicaragua's Caribbean coast, are a true tropical paradise. Comprising several small, unspoiled islands, these cays offer an escape to some of the most beautiful and serene beaches in the country.

- **Pristine Beaches and Waters**: Each cay in the Pearl Cays features its own pristine white sandy beach, fringed by crystal-clear, turquoise waters. These beaches are perfect for sunbathing, offering a tranquil environment to relax and unwind. The calm and clear waters also make the cays an ideal spot for snorkeling, where visitors can explore vibrant coral reefs and an abundance of marine life in the warm Caribbean Sea.
- **Access to the Cays**: The primary access to the Pearl Cays is by boat, typically from Pearl Lagoon. The journey itself is an adventure, offering stunning views of the coastline and the Caribbean Sea. Visitors can arrange boat trips through local tour operators in Pearl Lagoon, who offer various packages including day trips or longer stays. These tours often include stops at multiple cays, giving visitors the chance to experience the unique character of each.
- **Tour Operator Services**: Local tour operators not only provide transportation but can also offer additional services such as snorkeling gear rental and guided tours. Some packages might include meals or picnics, which is particularly convenient given the limited facilities on the cays.
- **Planning Your Visit**: When planning a trip to the Pearl Cays, it's important to consider the limited development on the islands. Visitors should come prepared with all necessary supplies, including sun protection, water, and snacks. It's also advisable to check weather conditions and sea forecasts before embarking on the journey, as these can affect boat travel.

A visit to the Pearl Cays is an opportunity to experience some of Nicaragua's most idyllic and untouched beaches. The tranquility and natural beauty of these islands make them a perfect destination for those looking to escape the hustle and bustle of everyday life and immerse themselves in a tropical paradise.

Jiquilillo

Jiquilillo is a hidden gem among Nicaragua's beach destinations, offering a more rustic and untouched seaside experience. This charming beach is known for its long stretch of dark sand and its serene, natural setting, making it an ideal spot for those seeking a quieter, more authentic coastal experience.

- **Tranquil Beach Atmosphere**: The beauty of Jiquilillo lies in its simplicity and tranquility. The expansive dark sand beach is less crowded than more popular tourist spots, providing a peaceful environment perfect for relaxation and contemplation. It's an excellent place for long, leisurely beach walks where you can enjoy the sound of the waves and the beauty of the ocean uninterrupted.
- **Activities and Experiences**: Jiquilillo's unspoiled nature lends itself to a variety of outdoor activities. Horseback riding along the beach is a popular activity, offering a unique way to explore the coastline. The beach's long stretches also make it ideal for jogging or playing beach games. The calm waters are suitable for swimming, and the sunsets here are particularly stunning, painting the sky in vibrant hues each evening.
- **Experiencing Rustic Nicaragua**: Visiting Jiquilillo is an opportunity to experience a more traditional and rustic side of Nicaragua's coastline. The area's laid-back vibe and natural beauty offer a glimpse into a lifestyle that is connected to the sea and the rhythms

of nature.

- **Parking and Village Amenities**: Jiquilillo is adjacent to a small beach village where parking is readily available. The village itself, though small, provides basic amenities and a chance to interact with the local community. Visitors can find modest accommodations and dining options, offering fresh seafood and local dishes.
- **Tips for Visitors**: Given its less developed nature, it's a good idea for visitors to come prepared with essentials like water, sun protection, and any specific beach gear. Embracing the simplicity of Jiquilillo is part of its charm, making it a perfect destination for those looking to disconnect and enjoy a more natural, serene beach environment.

Jiquilillo's allure lies in its unspoiled beauty and peaceful ambiance. It's a place where time seems to slow down, allowing visitors to savor every moment of their beach experience. For those seeking an escape from the more commercialized beach destinations, Jiquilillo offers a refreshing return to the basics of seaside enjoyment.

Miskito Cays

The Miskito Cays are a breathtaking archipelago located in the remote northeastern waters of Nicaragua, offering a unique and pristine experience for those looking to explore off the beaten path. These untouched coral islands are a haven for adventure and nature enthusiasts.

- **Remote and Pristine**: The Miskito Cays stand out for their unspoiled beauty and the sense of solitude they offer. The islands are relatively undeveloped, preserving their natural charm and appeal. This remoteness means fewer tourists and a more intimate

interaction with nature.
- **Activities and Marine Life**: The cays are a paradise for fishing, diving, and snorkeling enthusiasts. The surrounding waters are teeming with diverse marine life, making them an excellent spot for underwater exploration. The coral reefs around the islands are home to a colorful array of fish, sea turtles, and other marine creatures. For fishing aficionados, the waters offer the chance to catch a variety of fish in a serene and picturesque setting.
- **Accessing the Miskito Cays**: Reaching the Miskito Cays requires some planning, as they are not accessible by conventional means. The most common way to visit the cays is by arranging a boat trip from Puerto Cabezas, a town on the northeastern coast of Nicaragua. These trips are typically organized by local tour operators, who can provide tailored experiences, including day trips or longer stays with accommodations on the islands.
- **Tour Operator Services**: Given the remote location of the cays, it's advisable to use the services of a reputable tour operator. They can handle the logistics of transportation, guide you to the best spots for fishing or diving, and ensure a safe and enjoyable trip. These operators are also knowledgeable about the weather patterns and sea conditions, which is crucial for a safe journey to the cays.
- **Preparing for Your Visit**: When planning a trip to the Miskito Cays, it's important to be well-prepared. This includes bringing essential gear for your chosen activities, such as snorkeling or fishing equipment, as well as basic travel necessities like sun protection, water, and snacks. As the facilities on the cays are minimal, it's advisable to carry everything you might need for the duration of your visit.

Visiting the Miskito Cays is an adventure into a less-traveled part of Nicaragua, offering an unparalleled experience of tranquility, natural beauty, and rich marine life. For those seeking an authentic and secluded island experience, the Miskito Cays are a perfect destination.

Punta Jesus Maria

Punta Jesus Maria, located on the enchanting Ometepe Island in Lake Nicaragua, is a distinctive and captivating beach destination. This slender strip of land stretches out into the lake, providing visitors with a unique beach experience and breathtaking views.

- **Scenic Location**: The beach is particularly famous for its stunning vistas of Ometepe Island's twin volcanoes, Concepción and Maderas, which provide a majestic backdrop. The location of Punta Jesus Maria allows for panoramic views of these geological wonders, making it a photographer's delight and a perfect spot for those seeking picturesque natural scenery.
- **Beach Activities**: The gentle waters of Lake Nicaragua at this point make Punta Jesus Maria an excellent choice for swimming. The beach's extension into the lake creates a unique swimming experience, with clear, shallow waters ideal for both adults and children. Additionally, the beach's expansive area is perfect for picnicking, offering a serene setting for a relaxing day by the lake.
- **Entrance Fee and Facilities**: Access to Punta Jesus Maria requires a small entrance fee, which goes towards the maintenance and upkeep of the area. The beach is equipped with basic amenities, including picnic areas and sometimes vendors selling local snacks and drinks.
- **Parking**: Conveniently, there is parking available on-site at Punta Jesus Maria. The parking area is close to the beach, allowing easy access for unloading picnic supplies, swimming gear, and other essentials for a day at the beach.

- **Tips for Visitors**: When visiting Punta Jesus Maria, it's advisable to bring along any specific beach equipment you might need, such as beach chairs or umbrellas, as well as sun protection. Given its popularity, especially on weekends and holidays, arriving early to secure a good spot is recommended.

Punta Jesus Maria offers a unique beach experience, combining the tranquility of a lakeside setting with awe-inspiring volcanic views. Whether you're swimming in the calm waters, enjoying a lakeside picnic, or simply admiring the stunning landscape, Punta Jesus Maria provides a memorable and picturesque escape on Ometepe Island.

Each of these beaches showcases the diverse beauty of Nicaragua's coastline, offering everything from adventurous surf spots to tranquil tropical escapes. Whether you're looking to catch waves, soak up the sun, or explore unspoiled natural beauty, Nicaragua's beaches offer an array of experiences for every type of beachgoer.

7

Day Trips

N icaragua offers a plethora of day trip opportunities, each promising an array of experiences ranging from cultural immersions to natural explorations. This chapter outlines detailed itineraries for three different day trips, ensuring you capture some of the best experiences Nicaragua has to offer, including delicious food, exciting activities, picturesque viewpoints, beautiful beaches, and more.

Valle La Laguna Day Trip

Embark on a day of serene beauty and outdoor adventure with a trip to Valle La Laguna. This area, celebrated for its natural splendor and peaceful ambiance, offers a perfect escape into nature.

Morning: Hiking in Laguna de Apoyo Nature Reserve

- Begin your day with an early drive to the tranquil Laguna de Apoyo Nature Reserve.
- Engage in a light hike through this protected area, where you can immerse yourself in the lush surroundings and enjoy stunning views of the crater lake.
- Keep an eye out for local wildlife, including a variety of bird species, monkeys, and perhaps even the elusive sloth. The nature reserve is a haven for biodiversity, offering an opportunity to connect with nature.

Lunch: Lakeside Dining

- After your hike, visit one of the lakeside restaurants for a relaxing lunch. These eateries offer traditional Nicaraguan dishes made with fresh, local ingredients.
- Enjoy your meal with a view of Laguna de Apoyo, savoring the tranquility of the lake and its surrounding forest.

Afternoon: Water Activities on the Lake

- Spend your afternoon engaging in water activities on Laguna de Apoyo.
- Options include kayaking or paddleboarding, allowing you to explore the lake at your own pace. These activities offer a unique perspective of the lake and its natural beauty.
- Alternatively, you can choose to unwind by the lake, soaking in the sun, swimming in the clear waters, or simply enjoying the peaceful atmosphere.

<u>Evening</u>: Sunset at Catarina Viewpoint

- Conclude your day with a visit to the Catarina viewpoint, known for its panoramic vistas.
- The viewpoint offers a breathtaking sunset view over Laguna de Apoyo and the surrounding landscape. It's the perfect spot to reflect on your day's experiences and soak in the beauty of Nicaragua's natural landscapes.
- The Catarina viewpoint also has small shops and stalls, where you can pick up local crafts or enjoy a refreshing drink as the day winds down.

This day trip to Valle La Laguna offers a blend of hiking, dining, and relaxation, all set against the backdrop of one of Nicaragua's most beautiful natural areas. It's an ideal itinerary for those seeking a day of tranquility and outdoor enjoyment in a stunning natural setting.

Estelí Day Trip (Including Cigar Factory Tour)

Discover the cultural richness of Estelí, a city in northern Nicaragua known for its vibrant arts scene and renowned cigar industry. This day trip offers a blend of cultural exploration and natural beauty.

<u>Morning</u>: Cigar Factory Tour

- Start your day with an early departure for Estelí, a city that plays a significant role in Nicaragua's cigar industry.
- Upon arrival, embark on a guided tour of one of the city's esteemed cigar factories. This is a unique opportunity to witness firsthand the intricate process of cigar making, from leaf selection to rolling and aging.
- Learn about the historical and cultural importance of cigar production in Nicaragua and the craftsmanship that goes into creating

some of the world's finest cigars.

Lunch: Traditional Cuisine in Estelí

- For lunch, visit a local restaurant in Estelí to sample the traditional cuisine of northern Nicaragua. The region's dishes often feature hearty ingredients and rich flavors, offering a true taste of local culinary culture.
- Enjoy specialties like carne asada (grilled meat), gallo pinto (rice and beans), and other Nicaraguan staples, accompanied by fresh, locally-produced ingredients.

Afternoon: Exploring Estelí

- After lunch, take the time to explore the city's vibrant arts scene. Estelí is known for its stunning murals, many of which depict the country's history and culture. A walk through the city offers a visual journey through Nicaragua's past and present.
- Visit local artisan markets where you can find a variety of handmade crafts, offering a glimpse into the region's artistic talents. It's a great opportunity to pick up unique souvenirs and support local artisans.
- Optionally, if time permits, consider a short trip to the nearby Miraflor Nature Reserve, where you can enjoy the area's natural beauty and biodiversity.

Evening: Return Journey

- In the evening, begin your journey back to your base. Before you depart, consider stopping at a local café in Estelí for a cup of Nicaraguan coffee and a light snack. It's a perfect way to reflect on your day's experiences in the relaxed atmosphere of the city.

- As you return, enjoy the scenic drive, taking with you memories of a day filled with cultural insights, culinary delights, and the rich heritage of Estelí.

This day trip to Estelí offers a comprehensive experience of Nicaraguan culture, from its world-renowned cigar industry to its rich culinary traditions and vibrant arts. It's an ideal excursion for those looking to delve deeper into the cultural fabric of Nicaragua.

Granada Day Trip

A day trip to Granada, one of Nicaragua's oldest and most picturesque cities, is like stepping back in time. With its rich colonial history, vibrant street life, and stunning natural surroundings, Granada offers a day filled with exploration and discovery.

Morning: Exploring Colonial Granada

- Start your day with an arrival in Granada, a city that captivates with its colonial charm and historical significance.
- Embark on a walking tour of the city, where you can admire the colorful colonial architecture and visit key landmarks. The Granada Cathedral, with its striking yellow and white façade, is a must-see. Its interior is equally impressive and offers a peaceful retreat.
- Another significant stop is the San Francisco Convent and Museum, one of the oldest buildings in Central America, which houses an extensive collection of indigenous art and artifacts.

Lunch: Dining in the Central Square

- For lunch, choose one of the charming cafés in Granada's central square. Here, you can enjoy traditional Nicaraguan cuisine while watching the bustling city life. The central square is a lively hub of activity, offering a glimpse into the daily life of Granadians.

Afternoon: Boat Tour of the Isletas de Granada

- In the afternoon, take a relaxing boat tour of the Isletas de Granada, a group of small islands located in Lake Nicaragua. These islets are known for their natural beauty and the unique lifestyle of their inhabitants.
- The boat tour provides an opportunity to see a variety of flora and fauna, as well as to observe the luxurious private homes and small communities that exist on the islets. The tranquil waters and lush greenery make for a picturesque and serene experience.

Evening: Strolling and Dining on Calle La Calzada

- Before concluding your day trip, take a leisurely stroll along Calle La Calzada, a vibrant street known for its restaurants, bars, and live music. It's the perfect place to soak in the evening atmosphere of Granada.
- Choose one of the many restaurants for dinner, where you can savor local and international dishes. If time allows, enjoy a sunset view over Lake Nicaragua, adding a perfect end to your day in Granada.

A day trip to Granada is an immersion into the heart of Nicaraguan culture and history, combined with the natural beauty of its surroundings. It offers a perfect blend of historical exploration, culinary delights, and relaxation by the lake, making it a memorable and enriching experience.

San Juan del Sur Day Trip

A day trip to San Juan del Sur, a picturesque coastal town in Nicaragua, promises a delightful blend of scenic beauty, beach relaxation, and cultural exploration. Renowned for its stunning bay and vibrant atmosphere, San Juan del Sur is a perfect destination for a day of leisure and adventure.

Morning: Visit Cristo de la Misericordia

- Begin your journey with an early drive to San Juan del Sur.
- Start your exploration with a visit to the iconic Cristo de la Misericordia statue, one of the tallest Jesus statues in the world, situated atop a hill overlooking the town.
- The site offers panoramic views of San Juan del Sur Bay and the surrounding landscape, making it a perfect spot for photography and taking in the natural beauty of the area.

Lunch: Beachfront Dining

- For lunch, head to one of the many beachfront restaurants in San Juan del Sur. These eateries offer a range of options, from fresh seafood to traditional Nicaraguan dishes.
- Enjoy your meal with the picturesque backdrop of the bay, feeling the ocean breeze and soaking in the laid-back beach atmosphere.

Afternoon: Beach Time and Surfing Lessons

- Spend your afternoon on the beautiful beaches of San Juan del Sur. The town's main beach, with its golden sand and inviting waters, is ideal for relaxation and swimming.
- For those seeking a bit of adventure, San Juan del Sur is also a popular surfing destination. Take the opportunity to try out surfing with lessons available for beginners. The friendly instructors

will guide you through the basics, offering a fun and safe surfing experience.

Evening: Explore the Town and Dinner

- As the day begins to wind down, take a leisurely stroll through the colorful streets of San Juan del Sur. Explore the local shops, where you can find unique souvenirs and artisan crafts.
- Conclude your day trip with dinner at one of the town's local restaurants. It's a chance to reflect on your day's adventures and savor the flavors of Nicaraguan cuisine, rounding off a perfect day in this charming coastal town.

A day trip to San Juan del Sur offers a comprehensive experience of Nicaragua's coastal charm, from breathtaking views to beachside relaxation and cultural exploration. It's a destination that combines the best of natural beauty, leisure activities, and local culture, making it a must-visit for anyone traveling in Nicaragua.

Each of these day trips provides a glimpse into the diverse attractions Nicaragua has to offer, from its rich cultural heritage to its breathtaking natural landscapes. Whether you're a nature lover, a culture enthusiast, or simply seeking a relaxing day by the water, these itineraries offer something for every traveler.

8

Best Family Activities

N icaragua is a treasure trove of activities suitable for families and couples alike. From the thrill of volcano exploration to the charm of colonial cities, this chapter details a variety of activities that offer fun, adventure, and cultural immersion.

1. Volcano Exploration

- Masaya Volcano: Visit the active Masaya Volcano, where you can drive right up to the crater's edge and witness the bubbling lava below. It's both thrilling and educational.
- Cerro Negro: For an adventurous experience, hike up Cerro Negro

and try volcano boarding, a unique activity where you slide down the volcanic ash slopes.
- Mombacho Volcano: Explore the cloud forests of Mombacho Volcano on foot, enjoying the rich biodiversity and stunning views of Granada and Lake Nicaragua.

2. Beach Days

- San Juan del Sur: Spend a day at the popular San Juan del Sur beach, known for its beautiful bay and family-friendly atmosphere. Try surfing lessons or simply relax on the sand.
- Playa Hermosa: A quieter option, Playa Hermosa offers pristine sands and gentle waves, perfect for families with young children.
- Pearl Cays: Take a boat trip to the Pearl Cays for a day of snorkeling in crystal-clear waters and lounging on untouched beaches.

3. Colonial City Tours

- Granada: Wander the colorful streets of Granada, taking in sights like the Granada Cathedral and the Convento y Museo San Francisco.
- León: In León, visit the UNESCO-listed Cathedral of León, explore art galleries, and learn about the city's revolutionary history.
- Rivas: Discover the lesser-known colonial city of Rivas, with its rich history and charming central park.

4. Nature Reserves

- Indio Maíz Biological Reserve: Explore this lush rainforest reserve, home to a diverse range of wildlife including monkeys, sloths, and countless bird species.

- Chocoyero-El Brujo Natural Reserve: A perfect spot for bird watching, especially the Chocoyos (Parakeets) that reside near the waterfalls.
- Bosawás Biosphere Reserve: Venture into one of the largest rainforest reserves in Central America for an unforgettable eco-adventure.

5. Cultural Activities

- Pottery Making in San Juan de Oriente: Engage in a pottery-making workshop in this traditional pottery town.
- Dance Lessons: Take a family-friendly dance lesson in traditional Nicaraguan folk dance.
- Cooking Classes: Participate in a Nicaraguan cooking class, learning to make local dishes like gallo pinto or indio viejo.

6. Island Adventures

- Ometepe Island: Discover the twin volcanoes and petroglyphs on Ometepe Island, and enjoy kayaking in the Istián wetlands.
- Corn Islands: Experience Caribbean culture, beautiful beaches, and excellent snorkeling on the Corn Islands.
- Solentiname Archipelago: Explore this tranquil group of islands, famous for their artisan community and birdlife.

7. Water Sports

- Surfing at Maderas Beach: Perfect for beginners and experienced surfers, with surf schools available.
- Kayaking in Las Isletas: Paddle through the tranquil waters of Las Isletas in Lake Nicaragua.

- Scuba Diving at Corn Islands: Dive into the crystal-clear waters to explore vibrant coral reefs and marine life.

8. Coffee Farm Tours

- Matagalpa Region: Visit a coffee farm in the Matagalpa region to learn about coffee production and taste fresh coffee.
- Jinotega: Explore coffee plantations in Jinotega, known as the "Coffee Capital" of Nicaragua.
- Selva Negra: Tour the eco-friendly Selva Negra Coffee Estate and learn about sustainable coffee farming.

9. Local Markets

- Masaya Market: Shop for handicrafts and souvenirs at this vibrant market, known for its artisan products.
- Mercado Oriental in Managua: Experience the bustling atmosphere of one of Central America's largest markets.
- Catarina's Artisan Market: Enjoy beautiful views of Laguna de Apoyo while shopping for locally made crafts.

Each of these activities offers a unique way to experience Nicaragua's rich culture, beautiful landscapes, and wildlife, ensuring an enjoyable and memorable trip for families and couples alike. For a hassle free experience be sure to coordinate and schedule these activities with a tour company or someone from your hotel.

9

Best Surf Spots

Nicaragua, with its consistent offshore winds and variety of wave types, is a surfer's paradise. This chapter delves into the best surf spots across the country, highlighting what makes each location unique and the skill levels they cater to. Whether you're a seasoned pro or just starting out, Nicaragua's surf spots offer something for everyone.

1. The Boom

- **Location**: Northern Nicaragua
- **Skill Level**: Advanced

- **Unique Features**: Known for its powerful and heavy barrel waves, The Boom is a favorite among experienced surfers. The beach break here is fast and offers some of the best tubes in the country.
- **Tips**: Due to the intensity of the waves, it's recommended for skilled surfers only. The remote location means fewer crowds.

2. Lance's Left

    - **Location**: Near Astillero
    - **Skill Level**: Intermediate to Advanced
    - **Unique Features**: Lance's Left offers a long, consistent left-hand wave that provides an exhilarating ride. The spot is best known for its clean, smooth waves, ideal for those looking to improve their skills.
    - **Tips**: Best at mid to high tide, the spot can get crowded, so early morning sessions are recommended.

3. Popoyo Reef

    - **Location**: Tola
    - **Skill Level**: Intermediate to Advanced
    - **Unique Features**: This world-renowned break offers both left and right waves. Popoyo Reef is known for its reliability, with waves that hold well even on bigger swells.
    - **Tips**: The reef can be sharp, so booties are recommended. The area has several surf camps and schools.

4. Beginner's Bay

    - **Location**: San Juan del Sur
    - **Skill Level**: Beginner

- **Unique Features**: As the name suggests, Beginner's Bay is perfect for those just starting out. The waves here are smaller and more forgiving, making it an ideal spot for learning.
- **Tips**: There are plenty of surf schools in the area offering lessons and board rentals.

5. Playa Santana

- **Location**: Rivas Province
- **Skill Level**: All Levels
- **Unique Features**: Playa Santana is a versatile spot suitable for surfers of all skill levels. The beach break here produces both left and right waves that cater to different styles and abilities.
- **Tips**: The beach can get crowded, especially during peak season, so consider surfing during off-peak hours.

6. Colorados

- **Location**: Tola
- **Skill Level**: Advanced
- **Unique Features**: Colorados is famous for its fast and hollow barrel waves. The spot is a magnet for experienced surfers looking for a challenging ride.
- **Tips**: The waves here can be quite powerful, so it's not recommended for beginners. The best time to surf is during mid to high tide.

7. Playa Maderas

- **Location**: San Juan del Sur
- **Skill Level**: Beginner to Intermediate

- **Unique Features**: Playa Maderas is one of the most popular surf spots in Nicaragua, known for its consistent waves. It offers a variety of waves that cater to different skill levels.
- **Tips**: The beach is easily accessible and has a vibrant surf scene with plenty of surf schools, making it ideal for beginners and intermediates.

Each of these surf spots in Nicaragua offers unique waves and experiences, catering to a wide range of surfing preferences and skills. From challenging barrels to gentle waves perfect for beginners, Nicaragua's coastline is a surf enthusiast's dream. Remember to respect the local surf etiquette and enjoy the incredible surf that Nicaragua has to offer.

10

Conclusion

As our journey through the vibrant and diverse landscapes of Nicaragua comes to a close, it's clear that this beautiful country offers an abundance of treasures for every traveler. From the misty cloud forests and imposing volcanoes to the serene beaches and lively colonial cities, Nicaragua presents a world of adventure and cultural richness waiting to be explored.

Throughout this guide, we have traversed the length and breadth of Nicaragua, uncovering its hidden gems and well-loved spots. We've delved into the heart of its cities, ventured into the wilds of its nature reserves, savored the flavors of its traditional cuisine, and ridden the

CONCLUSION

waves of its renowned surf spots. Each experience has offered a unique insight into the spirit and charm of this enchanting country.

Nicaragua is a land where adventure meets tranquility, where history intertwines with vibrant contemporary culture, and where every sunset brings a promise of another unforgettable day. Whether you're a solo traveler seeking adventure, a family looking for a fun-filled vacation, or a couple in search of romantic escapades, Nicaragua promises memories that will last a lifetime.

As you return home, carrying with you the memories and experiences of this extraordinary journey, we hope that this guide has been your faithful companion, leading you to the wonders that Nicaragua holds.

Finally, if you have found this guide helpful in your Nicaraguan adventures, we would be incredibly grateful if you could take a moment to leave a review on Amazon. Your feedback not only helps us to improve but also guides fellow travelers in their journey to explore the magnificent country of Nicaragua. Share your stories, tips, and favorite moments – your insights are invaluable to the community of travelers and to the ongoing story of this wonderful country.

Thank you for choosing to explore Nicaragua with us, and we hope this journey has ignited a lifelong passion for discovery and adventure. Hasta luego, and may your travels always lead you to extraordinary places.

Keeping the Adventure Alive

Now that you've navigated the wonders of Nicaragua and have a treasure trove of insights at your fingertips, it's time to share your newfound knowledge with the world.

By taking a moment to leave your honest opinion of "Journey Through Nicaragua: Your Essential Guide to Top Attractions, Local Customs, and Must-See Activities for the Trip of a Lifetime" on Amazon, you'll guide other explorers to the same valuable resource you've enjoyed. Your review could be the compass that directs them to their next great adventure.

Thank you for your support. The spirit of exploration is kept alive when we pass on our tales and tips — and you're helping to keep that flame burning bright.

»> Click this link to leave your review on Amazon: https://qrco.de/jtnica

Your feedback not only enhances the journey for future travelers but also contributes to the global community of Nicaragua enthusiasts. Together, we can ensure that the beauty and excitement of Nicaragua continue to inspire adventurers for years to come.

11

Resources

Frommer, Arthur. "Ask Arthur Frommer: And Travel Better, Cheaper, Smarter". John Wiley & Sons, 2009, p. 329.

"Hotel La Polvora." Hotel La Polvora, www.hotellapolvora.com/. Accessed 15 Dec. 2023.

"El Guayacan Retreat." El Guayacan Retreat, www.elguayacanretreat.com/. Accessed 15 Dec. 2023.

"Visit Nicaragua." Visit Nicaragua, www.visitnicaragua.us/. Accessed 15 Dec. 2023.

"Cerro Negro Volcano." Visit Centro America, www.visitcentroamerica.com/en/visitar.

Accessed 15 Dec. 2023.

"Best Beaches in Nicaragua." Lonely Planet, www.lonelyplanet.com/articles/best-beaches-in-nicaragua. Accessed 15 Dec. 2023.

"Best Beaches in Nicaragua." Family Destinations Guide, www.familydestinationsguide.com/best-beaches-in-nicaragua/. Accessed 15 Dec. 2023.

"Granada, Nicaragua." Laid Back Trip, www.laidbacktrip.com/posts/granada-nicaragua. Accessed 15 Dec. 2023.

"Best Surf Spots in Nicaragua." Gathering Waves, www.gatheringwaves.com/best-surf-spots-in-nicaragua/. Accessed 15 Dec. 2023.

"Getting Around Nicaragua." Dream Big Travel Far, www.dreambigtravelfarblog.com/blog/getting-around-nicaragua. Accessed 15 Dec. 2023.

"Nine Nicaraguan Meals." Visit Nicaragua, www.visitnicaragua.us/2021/04/nine-nicaraguan-meals/. Accessed 15 Dec. 2023.

About the Author

Elena Carina Mendoza, an avid traveler and cultural enthusiast, has spent years immersing herself in the vibrant landscapes and rich traditions of Latin America. Born to a family of explorers, Elena's passion for discovery was ignited early in life. She grew up traversing diverse terrains, from the bustling streets of major cities to the serene expanses of rural countryside.

With a degree in Anthropology and Latin American Studies, Elena has a deep understanding of the intricate tapestries of culture and history that define the regions she explores. Her writing is fueled by a desire to unveil the authentic heart of each destination, going beyond the typical tourist trails to reveal the true essence of local life.

Elena's journey through Nicaragua, a country she describes as "a canvas of natural beauty and cultural richness," has been a transformative experience. Her travel guide on Nicaragua is not just a collection of recommendations; it's a narrative that weaves together the stories of the people, the flavors of the cuisine, and the rhythm of daily life.

When not on the road, Elena conducts workshops on sustainable travel and cultural preservation. She believes in traveling with purpose and respect for the places and people she visits. Through her writing and speaking, Elena Carina Mendoza inspires others to embark on their own journeys of discovery, with a mindful and open heart.

Printed in Great Britain
by Amazon